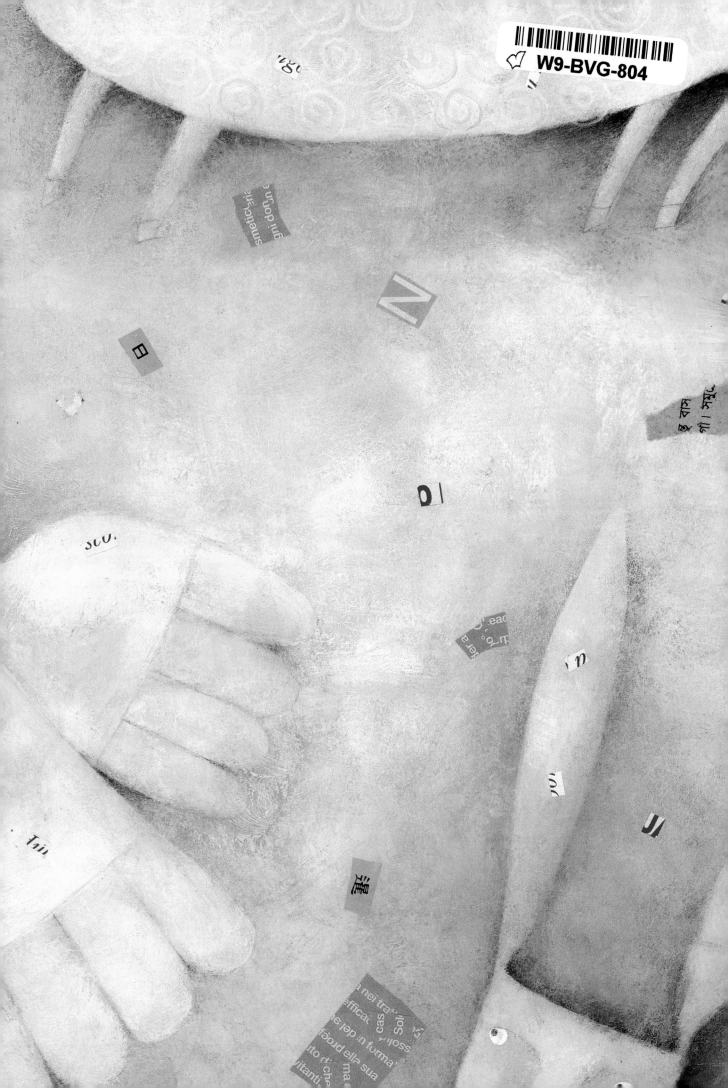

© Edizioni Arka, Milan, Italy 2003

This edition published 2004 in the United States of America by
Eerdmans Books for Young Readers
An imprint of Wm. B. Eerdmans Publishing Company
255 Jefferson SE, Grand Rapids, Michigan 49503
P.O. Box 163, Cambridge CB3 9PU U.K.
www.eerdmans.com

ISBN 0-8028-5279-3

04 05 06 07 08   6 5 4 3 2 1

Printed in Italy

Library of Congress Cataloging-in-Publication Data

Visconti, Guido.
One night in a stable / written by Guido Visconti ; illustrated by Alessandra
Cimatoribus.-- 1st ed.
p. cm.
Summary: An old ox makes room in his stable for all the animals in
need of shelter, as well as some unexpected travelers.
ISBN 0-8028-5279-3 (alk. paper)
[1. Animals--Fiction. 2. Jesus Christ--Nativity--Fiction.] I. Cimatoribus,
Alessandra, ill. II. Title.
PZ7.V8225On 2004
[E]--dc22
2004006808

One Night in a Stable

Written by Guido Visconti
Illustrated by Alessandra Cimatoribus

Eerdmans Books for Young Readers
Grand Rapids, Michigan • Cambridge, U.K.

One evening a strong
wind started blowing on
the hills surrounding
Bethlehem. While some
animals sought shelter
near the olive trees, one
lone dove flew under the
roof of a stable.

The ox that lived there was happy to see her. "I am old now and too tired to plough the fields anymore. I get terribly lonely in this stable," he told her. "Only my master comes to see me every now and then. Tell me, white dove, by any chance can you see him coming?"

"I'm afraid not," the dove replied. "I only see olive trees blowing in the wind and a cold little hare trying to find a burrow."

"Why don't you fly over to him and tell him to come to my stable? He'll find good shelter here," said the old ox.

And when the hare took refuge in the stable, the ox warmed him up with his strong breath.

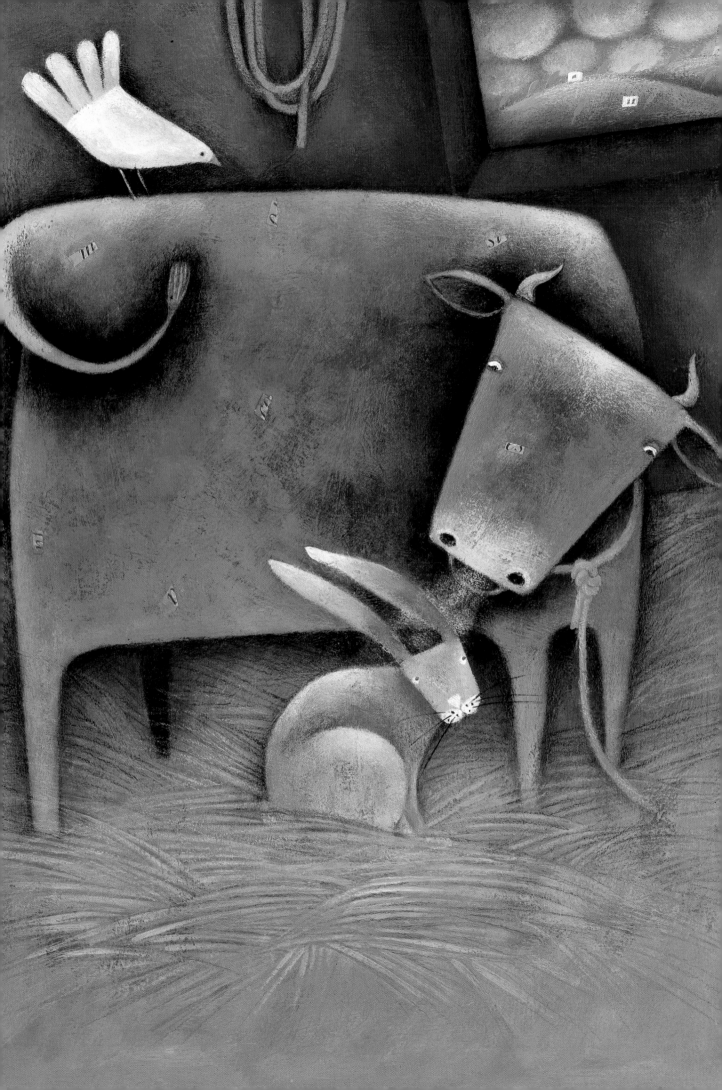

However, since the ox was hoping to see his master, once again he asked, "Tell me white dove, is there really no one approaching the stable?"

"I'm afraid not," replied the dove. "I only see the olive trees battling against the wind, large clouds covering the entire sky, and two lost little goats looking for their shepherd."

"There's lots of space in here. Tell them to come in too," said the old ox.

And when the goats took refuge in the stable, the ox warmed them up with his strong breath.

However, since he was still hoping to see his master, once again the ox asked, "Tell me, white dove, can you see anyone approaching the stable?"

"I'm afraid not," replied the dove. "I see only the windswept olive trees, where birds are gathering together against the cold of the snowflakes falling from the sky."

"Fly over to them and tell them to take shelter in here," said the ox, "or the snow will bury them."

When the birds felt the warmth of the stable spread through their wings, they started flying from one beam to the next. Hearing their birdsong, the old ox was filled with joy.

However, since his master kept him waiting, once more the old ox asked, "Tell me, white dove, is there no one at all approaching the stable?"

"I'm afraid not," said the dove. "I only see sheep under the olive trees trying to shake off the snow that is now falling fast."

"Fly to them and tell them there is still a little space in the stable," said the old ox. "It will be a bit crowded with all of us in here, but no one should have to stay outside on a cold night like tonight."

By the time the sheep had taken shelter in the warmth of the stable, night had fallen on the hills surrounding Bethlehem and on the stable among the olive trees. The ox, however, still had a small hope that his master would appear, and so once more he asked, "Tell me, white dove, can you see the quivering light of my master's lamp approaching in the darkness?"

"Yes, yes, I can see a light approaching," replied the dove excitedly, "but it's high up in the sky and it has left a sparkling trail behind it."

"It must be my master coming down the hill with a large torch in his hand. White dove, please, fly and tell him that I am waiting for him," rejoiced the old ox.

"No! No! I can't see your master. I can only see the bright light stopping over the stable," the dove cried.

Suddenly the wind ceased to blow. Then the voice of an angel outside the stable said, "There is an ox in this stable whose breath is strong and warm. While waiting for his master he offers shelter to everyone. A tired and heavily burdened donkey walking down the road will also come and need the ox's hospitality."

Silence fell inside the stable, and everyone heard the ox sigh. "The stable is too full now. There is no room left for another guest," he said sorrowfully.

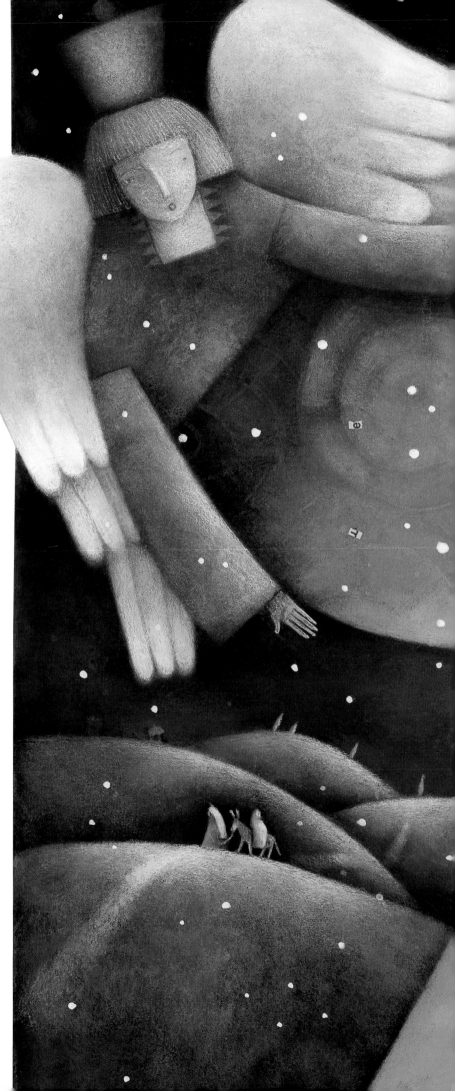

However, because his heart was full of love, the ox said to the dove, "Fly to the donkey and tell him that I'll give him my place. I'll break the rope that keeps me tied in, and I'll sleep outside in front of the door."

The ox, however, was old and very tired. He was trying in vain to break the rope when the stable door opened, pushed by a human hand. For a moment the ox was filled with joy, thinking that it was his master's hand. However, the voice asking if there was space for three more was not his master's!

"For four," cooed the dove excitedly. "Riding the donkey is a young woman who is about to give birth."

All in the stable were filled with joy. All, that is, except the ox. Once he would have been able to break the strongest chain but now he was no longer strong. Now he was a prisoner in his own stable, unable to offer shelter to a child who was about to be born.

"Don't worry. We'll make space for them," said the hare, the goats, and the sheep, leaving the stable one by one.

"If my master at least would come, he could free me from my rope. White dove, are you sure you don't see him coming?" asked the ox once more.

This time the dove made no reply. Only much later, when a cry was heard in the stable, she cooed softly: "I see a child laid in the straw. He is naked and needs your help."

The old ox lowered his eyes, and his heart suddenly filled with joy. He placed himself next to the child and warmed him with his strong breath.

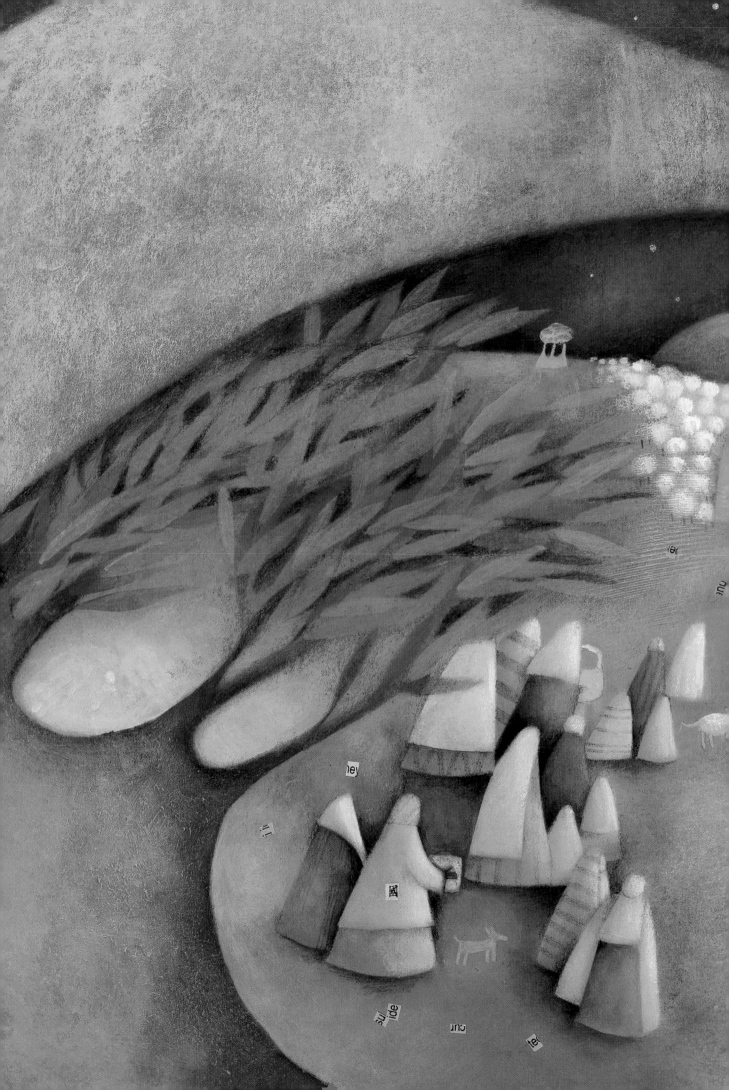

Only then did he hear his master's voice, deeply moved, saying to him, "Now you'll never feel lonely again in this stable. Farmers and shepherds are coming from the hills surrounding Bethlehem. They are coming to worship this child, who will forever be the new master of us all."

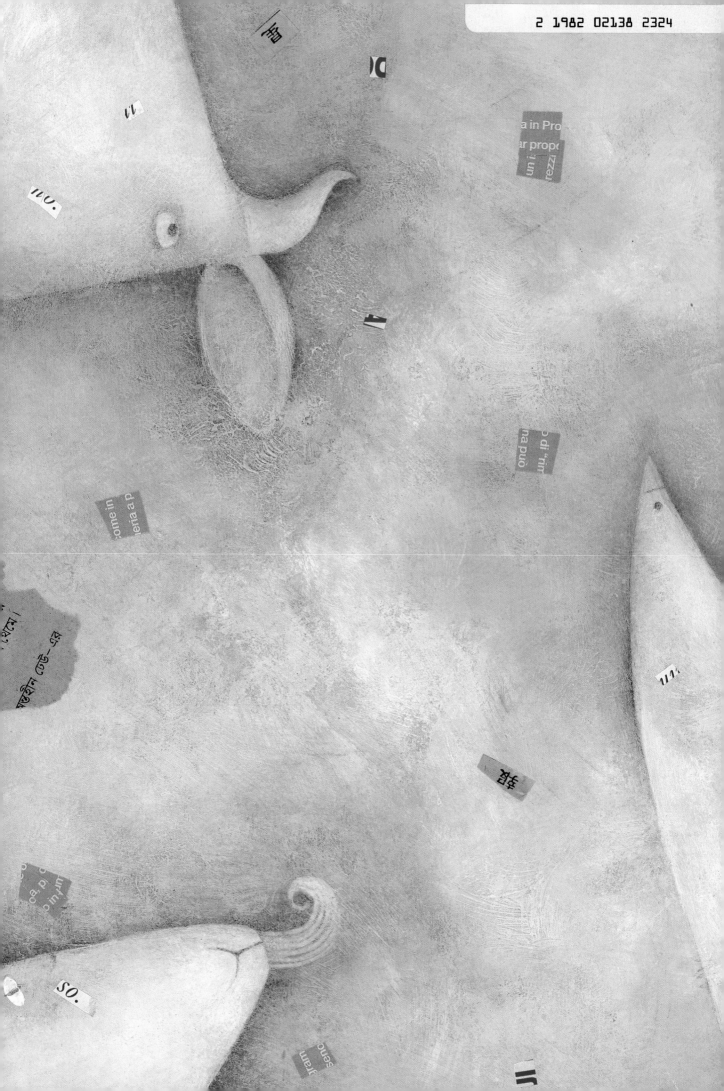